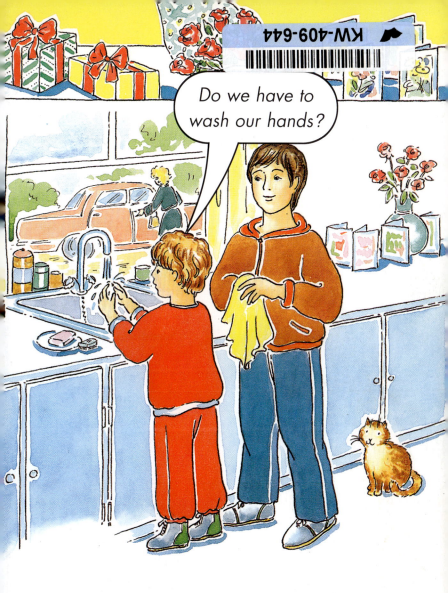

Yes, when you are preparing food
everything must be clean.

641.5

LEICESTERSHIRE
COUNTY COUNCIL
LIBRARIES AND
INFORMATION SERVICE

641.5

MOUNTFIELDS LODGE PRIMARY SCHOOL
EPINAL WAY
LOUGHBOROUGH LE11 0QE
TEL: 01509 214119

Redmayne
Ann

Cold cooking

Charges are payable on books overdue at public libraries. This book is due for return by the last date shown but if not required by another reader may be renewed — ask at the library, telephone or write quoting the last date and the details shown above.　　　　G3

04017

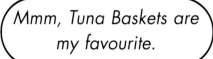

Mmm, Tuna Baskets are my favourite.

I like Strawberry Ice Cream and so does Mum.

Food which needs to be cooled or frozen must be made first. The ice cream should be made first, even though it will be eaten last.

7

STRAWBERRY ICE CREAM

Ingredients

500g of strawberries or other
soft fruit in season

50g of icing sugar

100ml of water

285ml of double cream

Utensils

2 medium bowls
1 large bowl
fork
balloon whisk

measuring jug
spoon
freezer container
sundae dishes

10

*Can I scrape
out the bowl?*

The ice cream will be ready to eat after
three hours in the freezer.

SUNFLOWER CHEESE

Ingredients

1 tin containing 8 pineapple rings

5 small lettuce leaves

225g of cream cheese

40g of walnut pieces

cucumber

Utensils

tin opener

cup

1 bowl

2 spoons

kitchen knife

5 medium plates

12

The edges of a tin can be sharp.
You should always get an adult to
open tins for you.

13

Always wash fruit and vegetables before eating them to be sure that they are clean.

Now I'll put a spoonful of cheese into the middle of each pineapple ring.

16

Nuts are tasty to eat and good for you.
They are also used as decoration.
When food is decorated like this, it
is called garnishing.

17

TOMATO TUNA BASKETS

Ingredients

5 large tomatoes

185g tin of tuna in oil or brine

150g of natural yoghurt

Utensils

kitchen knife

medium bowl

small spoon

tin opener

fork

serving plate

18

21

I'm piling the mixture back into the tomatoes...

...and I'm putting the lids back on.

22

Arrange the tomatoes carefully on a large serving dish. You must make sure they will not fall over.

When food looks interesting, it's more fun to eat.

23

TOSSED SALAD

Ingredients

half a lemon

1 apple

a few radishes

2 spring onions

a crisp lettuce

a head of broccoli

Utensils

lemon squeezer

kitchen knife

colander

2 small bowls

large salad bowl

pair salad servers

If you dip the chopped apple into
lemon juice it will stop the apple
pieces going brown.

25

Choose your salad ingredients for their different flavours, colours and textures.

I'll break the broccoli into pieces.

Raw food, like salad, has more vitamins and minerals than cooked food.

27

HONEY AND
MINT DRESSING

4 tbsp of cider vinegar

3 tbsp of olive oil

2 tbsp of clear honey

several mint leaves or half a tsp
of dried mint

salt and pepper

Utensils

small screw-topped jar | tablespoon

This salad dressing is easy to make.

We just put everything into the jar...

...and then shake it all up.

Dressings add exciting flavours to salad.
Pour the dressing over the salad and
mix together just before serving.

29

Can you remember the names of the dishes the children have prepared for Mum's birthday tea?

30